Numbskulls
Navigating Personality Conflicts

Numbskulls: Navigating Personality Conflicts

Jon Coley

Published by Jon Coley, 2023.

While every precaution has been taken in the preparation of this book, the publisher assumes no responsibility for errors or omissions, or for damages resulting from the use of the information contained herein.

NUMBSKULLS: NAVIGATING PERSONALITY CONFLICTS

First edition. May 15, 2023.

Copyright © 2023 Jon Coley.

ISBN: 979-8223989165

Written by Jon Coley.

This book is dedicated to my wonderful and patient coworkers. Thank you all for putting up with my personality typobsession.

Jon Coley

Table of Contents

Thank you to Carol and Durand for helping me get this book right.

1. Introduction

Honesty is the single most important factor having a direct bearing on the final success of an individual, corporation, or product.

-Ed McMahon

We've all been there, dealing with that kid you just can't reach, or with that coworker who doesn't really get you. Maybe it's that family member who always gives you a hard time. Whether it's a teacher-student relationship or an impossible colleague, we all have personality conflicts from time to time. It's like dealing with a numbskull. Well, during the moment of conflict, that's exactly what all these people are, total numbskulls. It's okay, though. There are easy to understand psychological reasons for this. By the way, sometimes you are he numbskull too, no offense. But what if there were a way to circumvent the power struggle, or at least reset the conversation?

This book attempts to help you navigate your way through personality conflicts by using observations found in personality typology. Specifically, we are looking at three phenomena; cognitive functions, blind spots, and the inferior function grip. Also, the primary strategy to be used is a modified version of the linguistic phenomenon called code switching. So when waters get dangerous, perhaps there is a way to observe and recognize the language being used, and then switch up the dominant thought patterns taking place during a power struggle or some other uncomfortable conversation. In other words, there may be a way to navigate through the choppy areas, and to sail on into those blessed calmer waters.

Since the aim of this book is to be as useful and practical as possible, not too much time is going to be spent on personality theory. We are not going to worry too much about recognizing personality types or diving deep into how personality typing works. That's for another book. I already wrote one of those, by the way.

Instead, we are going to take a quick look at the eight cognitive functions as described by MBTI (Myers-Briggs Type Indicator). Next, there will be a brief discussion of the cognitive blind spot as understood from the Socionics system (basically the USSR version of MBTI). Rounding out the theory portion of the book is a description of the inferior function grip phenomenon. While entire articles could be written about each of the things above (and tons of YouTube videos produced), we're going to skim the surface rather quickly and go straight to the main strategy, code switching. Rest assured, this is not at all a difficult concept. No worries, folks, this won't be a brain stretching book. Once we've gotten all that tedious prep work out of the way, we can finally begin dealing with all those numb skulls. Who knows, you may be able to. Are yourself a little less numbskullish (totally made up word) in the bargain.

2. Cognitive Functions

It's better to be an octopus than a fish. If an octopus loses a tentacle to a predator, the octopus will survive with seven tentacles left to itself.

-Gene Simmons

There are eight cognitive functions in the MBTI system. Each personality type uses four of them. The other four are latent and are placed in what Carl Jung referred to as the Shadow. From there, Socionics picked up on the shadow functions and the blind spot, but more on that later. The four active functions make up a personality type. They are ordered in what's called a cognitive stack, which is like a simplified map of the brain. The order of preference ranges as follows: primary, secondary, tertiary, and inferior. There is a lot more to it than this, but a full understanding of the personality typing system is not the mission of this book. This chapter, instead, provides brief descriptions of each of the eight cognitive functions. Understanding what they are and how to recognize them is the key to navigating personality conflicts. Knowledge is power.

The Judging Functions

The judging functions are the thinking patterns people use to make decisions and judgments. They come in two flavors, thinking and feeling. Each of the two flavors come in two packages, introverted or extroverted. All you math wizards reading this paragraph have already figured out that there are four judging functions in total. The four judging functions are EXTROVERTED THINKING, INTROVERTED THINKING, EXTROVERTED FEELING, and

INTROVERTED FEELING. Each personality type is going to prefer one flavor over the other. Moreover, if the preferred flavor is extroverted, the other function will be less developed and introverted, or vise versa. For example, my own preferred judging function is introverted thinking (Ti), so my other judging function, which is the least developed in my cognitive stack is extroverted feeling (Fe). But enough about me, let's get into the proverbial nitty gritty.

The Thinking Functions

Introverted thinking (Ti) uses inward focused logic, which can be subjective or objective in nature, to make decisions. It understands and categorizes the way things are and how systems work. It is comprehension oriented and uses inductive reasoning, allowing for the integration of new data on a constant basis.

Extroverted thinking (Te) uses outward focused logic (usually objective) to make decisions. It organizes and instructs the outside world, things and people alike, into working systems. It is results and fairness oriented. It's deductive in nature, assuming a constant set of data in the outside world.

The Feeling Functions

Introverted feeling (Fi) makes decisions based on inward focused personal core values and emotions. It is also a value based filter of understanding the world. It is focused on authenticity and integrity.

Extroverted feeling (Fe) makes decisions based on the emotional atmosphere and common values of the tribe. It is focused on harmony and common happiness, or what's best for everyone involved.

Before moving on, it must be stated that all feelers think and all thinkers feel. Watch any MBTI YouTube video channel and you will eventually here that statement. To clarify, thinkers resort to logic first when making decisions by default. Feelers resort by default to values or feelings first. Both personality types can move across the aisle, so to speak, to make better informed decisions. For example, I'm an ISTP. If I were a project manager in charge of a group, I would be inclined to make assignments based on logic. (Tammy is better at a certain skill, so she should do job A.) However, my logical decisions can be influenced by values too. (Tammy is tired of doing that kind of work and others could do it almost as well. Since I value Tammy's feelings, perhaps she should do job B for this project.) We'd better move on now. I'm talking about myself again, and I have no idea who Tammy is.

The Perceiving Functions

The perceiving functions are the thinking patterns that your brain uses to take in data and information from the outside world. There are two general perceiving modes. The first is sensing, which is more concrete and detail oriented. The second is intuition, which is more abstract and pattern or connection oriented. Once again there are two attitudes for both modes, introverted and extroverted. This comes to two times two, which equals four. Hence we have the final four cognitive functions.

Just like the judging functions, your preferred perceiving function is higher in the cognitive stack. Your other function is lower in the stack and will have the opposite attitude. If you prefer extroverted sensing (Se), then introverted intuition (Ni) will be lower in the stack, and less developed. Or, like Willy Wonka, you can scratch that and reverse it.

The Sensing Functions

Extroverted Sensing (Se) is probably the easiest of all to understand. It takes in vast amounts of detailed information from the outside world using the five senses. But wait, there's more. Since most people do this, it would seem to be a cognitive function everyone uses. This is not the case. Extroverted Sensing uses the five senses plus the other lesser known senses like balance, temperature, and proprioception. High Se users are placed firmly in present reality far more than people with other personality types.

Introverted Sensing (Si) also takes in large amounts of concrete detailed information through the five senses in real time. However, it also simultaneously compares that information to the past, or to the perceived way things ought to be. This happens automatically and often subconsciously. Hi Si users depend highly on their strong powers of memory.

The Intuitive Functions

Extroverted Intuition (Ne) focuses on the outside world and continually explores abstract patterns and connections. Hi Ne users are able to experiment with intellectually complex scenarios and discover insights that most would think to be completely random. Personality types with this function are able to discuss complicated and abstract ideas with seemingly little to no effort.

Introverted Intuition (Ni) focuses internally on perceived patterns or even gut feelings, and extrapolates them into the future. Hi Ni users are often able to predict with amazing certainty future events based on the connections they have made with current information. Moreover, they are able to glean deep insights into the nature of people, things, or situations that most cannot see.

The descriptions above are quite oversimplified. It has been said that the brain is the most complex creation in the universe. These eight functions don't even skim the surface. That having been said, they are still extremely useful. Additionally, they all come with a a language code that is easy to recognize if you're a keen observer. In short, much like the way body language experts can see more about what a person is saying, knowledge of cognitive functions can help you understand more about where the people in your tribe are coming from and who they really are. That's powerful knowledge to have.

Personality Types

There are sixteen personality types in the MBTI and the Socionics systems. While this book will not explore each one, it would be prudent to explain how the cognitive functions work together to form one personality type. I'll go with the one I know best - mine. Sorry, I have to talk about myself one more time.

I'm an ISTP, which stands for Introverted-Sensing-Thinking-Perceiving. The nicknames given to this type is The Crafter, The Mechanic, or The Virtuoso. These four letters are actually a code that unlocks my cognitive stack, the simplified schematic to my brain. My primary function is Introverted Thinking (Ti). My secondary function is Extroverted Sensing (Se). The tertiary function is Introverted Intuition (Ni). Finally, the inferior function is Extroverted Feeling (Fe). All the rest of my cognitive functions are relegated to my Shadow, but the seventh function is my blind spot, Extroverted Intuition (Ne).

The paragraph above probably reads like stereo instructions. There are other, more brain friendly ways, to explain this. I like to use a sailing ship metaphor.

We are all just ships sailing in a great big harbor. The captain of my ship is Ti, making logical decisions based on the knowledge at hand. The navigator of the ship is Se, keeping the captain informed of all the sailing conditions and helping to steer the ship correctly. The crew, which does less decisions making, but is responsible for keeping the ship in shape, is Ni. They can see things from a different perspective too, since they are not responsible for guiding the vessel. The last function is the passenger. Mine is Fe, focused on the ambience and morale of the ships in the harbor. It makes no decisions at all, but definitely has its opinions and isn't afraid to let them be known. All the other functions are below deck in the cargo hold. Deep down inside, there's a crate containing the blind spot function, which is Ne for me. It's my own personal numbskull cognitive function.

The metaphor above can be used to describe all sixteen personality types. If this interests you, I recommend reading my book, FROM THE PEANUTS SECTION: HOW A PERSONALITY PSYCHOLOGY NERD SEES EDUCATION. It contains detailed descriptions of each of the sixteen MBTI personality types, not just mine. There is also a thriving MBTI community on social media and YouTube. You should check that out as well.

But let's get back to the numbskulls. The next chapter will delineate the primary strategy for using personality psychology to navigate conflicts, which is the main purpose of this writing. While, like most things in life, it may be easier said than done, the plan is simple and easy to understand. Like MBTI itself, it's accessible to anyone who wants to give it a try. So let's pull up those anchors and set sail. The harbor awaits.

3. Strategy

Victory belongs to the most persevering.

-Napoleon Bonaparte

This strategy rocks. Okay, this strategy R-K-C-S. When faced with a personality conflict, there are three steps to take for successful navigation. R - Recognizing the kind of language the other person is using. If you know the person well, this is can be super easy. K - Knowing which cognitive function the person is using. If the person is upset, it may be the inferior function. If you're not getting through to the person, the problem may be the blind spot. CS - Code switching is the act of changing your language to fit the situation. Try to use language that fits another cognitive function. Continuing with the ship metaphor, this like the act of dropping a sail or turning a rudder. It provides a stable way out of the conflict and into more productive conversation.

Since we are in danger of having an incredibly short chapter, the paragraph above should probably be unpacked. Let's start with R. It is now time for us to recognize.

So you're in a disagreement or conflict with a coworker. The first step is to make a mental note recognizing the kind of language being used in the argument. Sure, if the moment is heated, this may be difficult, but it can be done. It takes some mental discipline to reserve the brain power for the mental task, but understanding the nature of the argument is a vital part of being able to navigate through it. Remember, though, that you only need to take a brief inventory in your mind. You don't have to analyze every word being said. Otherwise you risk analysis paralysis. All that you really need is to get a general overview, a bigger perspective.

Now let's move on to K - knowing the cognitive function in use. There are eight cognitive functions, which were discussed in the previous chapter. The type of language being spoken during the conflict is the key to knowing which cognitive function is being used. Also, it's important to note whether or not the person is emotional or upset at the time. This helps you to determine whether to avoid the other person's blind spot, or if the person is in the grip of his or her inferior function. All this will also be discussed in later chapters.

CS stands for code switching. This is something people do all the time without even thinking about it. The most famous example given in linguistic circles is black Americans, who talk one way when surrounded by peers of their same race, but change their speech patterns when in mixed company, especially in a professional setting. This is second nature to them. In most cases, they don't even realize they're doing it at the time. Some erroneously believe this is the only or the main example of the phenomenon. However, people are code switching all the time, regardless of race or ethnicity. Kids speak one way with each other, but change their speech patterns when speaking with adults, for example. The modified version of code switching recommended here is not changing speech patterns or accents for social situations, but changing sentence patterns to match the back and forth conversation as it relates to cognitive functions. Don't worry. It's far easier than it sounds. For instance, you can tell when someone is using heart, or feeling, language as opposed to head, or intellectual language. That being the case, you can code switch accordingly, though you are not used to speaking or thinking that way.

Okay, the prep work has been done. In the next chapter, we will dive right into those numbskulls' brains. Most of the rest of the book will be organized by the blind spot cognitive functions of the sixteen personality types. Once again, it is not necessary to type someone, though that can be helpful. It's not even necessary to know anything about the sixteen types in general. All that you need to know is the RKCS method. That being said, I do recommend learning about the MBTI system. There is a lot of insight that can be gleaned from it. The other systems, like The Big Five and The Enneagram are helpful too. MBTI just happens to be the one I prefer and trust the most. All of them do have their benefits. At any rate, we have the background information that we need, so let's move on to the good stuff. We have a lot of territory to cover and quite a few heads to crack, metaphorically speaking of course.

4. The Te Blind Spot

People couldn't understand why my mama would have a blind kid out doing things like cutting firewood. But her thing was: He may be blind, but he ain't stupid.

-Ray Charles

Before we dive in to the scenarios head first with no abandon, let's talk about pronouns. Some readers may notice that I change the pronouns pretty regularly in the next few chapters. This is not to be politically correct, which is a good thing, because that skill is not in my repertoire of abilities. Sometimes I try to assign the gender of a type based on how likely the person would be male or female in the population. These numbers are not equally distributed, nor are they particularly particularly reliable. It depends on whom you ask, and on which day of a given week it happens to be. For others, I happen to have a personal acquaintance in mind. That having been said, I don't think the following scenarios should be too confusing, so let's jump in.

There are two types with extroverted thinking (Te) being their blind spot, and they are Charlie Brown and Lucy. That may be a little too specific. The ISFJ personality type (Charlie Brown) is known as THE DEFENDER. The INFJ (Lucy) is called THE COUNSELOR. The former is considered one of the most common personality types, and the latter is the rarest. Be that as it may, they both have introverted thinking (Ti) in the third slot of their cognitive stack. To find the blind spot, change the attitude or focus of the tertiary function. In other words, Ti becomes Te, so the blind spot is extroverted thinking. Again, this book doesn't cover the cognitive stack in detail, or give descriptions of each personality type. You'll just have to trust me. But hey, I've never lied to you, have I? The most important thing is to be able to recognize when extroverted thinking isn't working with someone. If you would like to learn more about each personality type, I've totally got you covered. In the final pages of this book, I have a list of my other nonfiction work available, just saying.

Extroverted thinking (Te) is outward focused logic. It's creating systems, organizing the outside world, and making things work. It's telling people what to do too. The ISFJ doesn't react well to this. It can fill her (sometimes him) with angst. The INFJ usually doesn't react to this kind of thinking and behavior at all. THE COUNSELOR knows the real you, and is not impressed with your system, organization, or authority.

To navigate through this personality conflict, you will need to code switch, to speak their language. Both personality types are high Fe users (extroverted feeling). They are more interested in what it takes to boost the morale of the tribe. Additionally, they are focused on harmony. If you can change your language from Te to Fe, the both of them would be far more responsive. Try to change your line of thought from something like, "You do this and the work will get done," to something along the lines of, "You are the best choice for doing this because we can trust and depend on you to do it well and make us all look good." You don't have to lay it on that thick. Authenticity is required, but you get the picture.

It must be stated, however, that if you are a high Te user, you do not have Fe in your cognitive stack. Instead, you have introverted feeling (Fi). This doesn't mean you can't communicate using Fe, though. Unless it is your blind spot, you can switch from an efficiency focused mindset to a harmonizing thought pattern, at least for a little while. Remember, you're navigating through a personality conflict, not being untrue to yourself.

Okay, now let's switch gears. You're a manager and these two people come to you upset, hopefully not at the same time. They will each be caught in the "inferior grip." This means that they are distraught and their mind is caught in a rut, for lack of a better word. The thinking patterns would be consistent with the characteristics found in the fourth slot of their cognitive stacks. This cognitive function is the least developed active function of the personality, thus it is the inferior function. Since it's the least developed of the four, it reacts emotionally and negatively when things go awry. But these are two distinct personality types. While they have a common blind spot, they have two different inferior functions.

Let's begin with THE DEFENDER, the ISFJ, good old Charlie Brown. He comes to you upset in the grip of his inferior function, extroverted intuition (Ne). Oh boy, this will be quite a trip. He will be discussing all kinds of random things and jumping to wild conclusions about them. Of course they will be negative in nature, because he's upset. Before you do any code switching, let's discuss what you shouldn't do, contradict him. Telling him he's wrong will only make him feel worse, thus reinforcing the Ne grip.

Before we take care of Charlie Brown, let's deal with Lucy, the INFJ, or THE COUNSELOR. To be honest with you, she probably won't come to you at all. You will probably come to her and she'll be in a mood. It's up to you to notice that's she's in her inferior grip. Her inferior function is extroverted sensing (Se). If she's upset, she'll be spouting out a lot of concrete, negative details. INFJ's are intuitive creatures, details are not their strong suits. But even if you know that every single detail is erroneous, it will do you absolutely no good to mention that. She's in the Se grip, so you need to code switch.

Well, we've got two people with problems. The good news is that they both require one solution, harmony. Since their blind spot is Te, you already know that both of these types are high Fe users. You need to speak the language of extroverted feeling. Your focus should be on the outer tribe and how the morale or ambience is being affected. That's what both of these two types care most about, so you should focus on how this person contributes to the morale of the company, to the harmony of the office family. Since they are usually focused on and concerned about the well being of the tribe, it would be wise to let them know that you recognize their importance in this way. Listen to their complaints, wrong or right, and acknowledge them.

"I will look at how so-and-so is misusing the hedge mcglobber, but I want you to understand that we all depend on you and your work. You make things better around here. I know you're upset right now, but I think you've helped me see how to make things better for everyone."

Now before you go thinking the wrong thing, I don't in any way mean that you should appease them just to make them feel better. You should always be truthful and authentic. If you're not, they will both know it, especially the INFJ. Be truthful with them both. Take the time to actually think about the morale of the office, the tribe, or the family. While they may be wrong about the details (Se) or jumping to wild conclusions (Ne), they are probably right about the morale of the tribe being lowered in some way. A true Fe focus on your part will validate them and help them out of their inferior grips. Everyone will feel better and you will probably end up making the work environment a better place in the bargain.

The scenario above assumed a management-subordinate position. Of course, peers have personality conflicts too. The good news is that code switching doesn't depend on hierarchal position. Anyone can do it just as effectively as anyone else. Don't be afraid to give it a try. It's a lot better than arguing and bickering, or worse, clamming up with festering resentment, unless that's your idea of a good time. Also, keep in mind that people in their inferior grips are basically beside themselves. They are not in their right minds, but this is a temporary condition. That's why you can navigate these situations safely and perhaps create a win-win situation.

5. The Ne Blind Spot

A strong spirit transcends rules.

-Prince

Okay, stop me if you've heard this one. Schroeder and a Prince walk into a bar. They should have been watching where they were going.

The ISTP and the ISFP share the blind spot, extroverted intuition (Ne). Schroeder from the Peanuts franchise is a good example of the ISTP, or THE CRAFTER. Prince and John Denver are good ISFP, or THE ARTIST exemplars.

Extroverted intuition is outward focused, abstract exploration. It perceives and explores connections between what many people would presume to be random items, situations, and concepts. But it's not just connections between everyday objects and people, or even the random novel concept; it explores similarities and characteristics of ideas, scenarios and principles. It's brainstorming to the Nth degree. ISFP's and ISTP's are not fans of this cognitive function. They are grounded, down to earth people who have no time for such navel gazing. Yes, I'm even talking about The Purple One.

So you're in a meeting, kicking ideas and scenarios around. You're trying to get people over to your side, but the ISTP is rolling his eyes and the ISFP has clammed up and begun writing calligraphy on her notepad. What can you do to bring them back? If you happened to have been using extroverted intuition, which is likely if you're running a brainstorming session, it may be time to code switch. These two personalities are quite different from one another. One has introverted thinking (Ti) as a primary function, and the other has introverted feeling (Fi). No worries, they both have extroverted sensing (Se) high in their cognitive stacks. They share introverted intuition (Ni) too, but you likely don't have that function on the ready, given the fact that you have been using extroverted intuition in this scenario.

It's time to come back down to earth. Change your language so that you are focusing on more concrete details and actions. Also it's good to limit your focus to two or three, but not too many more, subjects at a time. You will need to Stop bouncing around so much. High Se users are planted firmly in present reality. They appreciate good, manifestly workable, and elegant solutions. If you can narrow your scope a little, they can more readily be brought back into the fold. This is a good thing, you want people like these on your side. Once good decisions are made, they can get things done.

Before moving on, both of these types are introverts. It is unlikely that they will come to you when upset. They both would prefer to work out their problems alone, generally speaking. With this in mind, the following scenario may be more like a chance encounter in the workplace, or perhaps a yearly review. At any rate, let's see what these two types are like in a disturbed state. Once again, it's not important that you know their personality types (though that is helpful). It is, however, far more useful for you to recognize the kind of language being used.

The ISTP personality type has extroverted feeling (Fe) in the inferior function slot. A more developed Fe function is focused on harmony and the needs of the tribe. A less developed version of this function would be reactive to negative morale. When in the Fe grip, the person may believe that nobody cares about him or her, or that they think little or ill of him. When you hear language like that, it's not time to contradict, but to reestablish reality. This personality type is usually not at all concerned about feelings, so an alarm bell should be ringing in your head. In short, it is time for code switching.

The ISFP personality type has extroverted thinking (Te) in the inferior function slot of the cognitive stack. Well developed Te is good at allocating responsibilities, being fair and logical, and developing systems that work like well oiled machines. A less developed Te is going to be focused on everything that is going wrong in the world around it. The distraught ISFP in the Te grip will be talking about how the (personal) world is falling apart, or how the system is breaking down. She will probably be is dismay about being helpless to do anything about it. Argument is pretty much always futile when people are in the grip of their inferior functions. The language needs to change.

Both of these types have extroverted sensing (Se) as their secondary function. While this function is considered the easiest to understand, most don't always recognize the language pattern associated with it. It involves concrete, real world in real time, detailed information. Ground these people back in reality if you can. It's where they usually live, far more than most other types. Don't waste time telling them that what they are saying isn't true. Instead, point out what is true about their situations, even down to the color of the chair in which they are sitting. Let them know you are really hearing what they are saying in no uncertain terms. You are not making their problems go away, but you are helping them to refocus their attention on the real things and situations around them and to reaffirm their places in the world. In other words, you want to help them find their metaphorical anchors again. Finally, they will probably want to be alone to work things out for themselves. You should respect that.

6. The Se Blind Spot

Big sisters are the crab grass in the lawn of life.

-Linus Van Pelt

Do you ever feel like you're talking to someone who's basically not existing on the same plane as everyone else? Do you ever feel like you're that person? As a kid someone may have asked, "What's the weather like on your planet?" Well, this may be why. There are two personality types that have extroverted sensing (Se) as their blind spots. This cognitive function grounds people in present reality, ergo the INTP and the INFP are both known for living in their own heads. Known as THE LOGICIAN (or THE ARCHITECT) and THE HEALER respectively, these two types are arguably best portrayed by Charles Schultz' two characters, Marcy and Linus.

Extroverted sensing (Se) is outward focused perception of concrete details in the real world through the five senses. Pretty much everyone does this, but high Se users depend on this function to continually ground themselves in moment, in present reality. Also, they more are in tune with the lesser senses, like balance, proprioception, temperature, and even air pressure. They are completely plugged in, but the IXFP's are completely unplugged.

INTP's and INFP's are both blind to this function, which leaves them in what some would consider a day dreaming state, but one should not be fooled into thinking that they are listless. Instead, they're almost always in deep, profound thought. Yes, there are really people out there like this. They are usually called nerds. Sometimes they are poets, philosophers or even mad scientists. Rest assured, we need them around us just as much as any other personality type. It takes all kinds.

So you're in a meeting and trying to get something done, but there's a member of the team who isn't on the same vibe as everyone else. Either he's waxing philosophical when it's time to get down to brass tacks (like Linus), or she's still throwing out barely connected pieces of abstract data (Marcy). It's time for solutions now, so you've got to move things along. It won't do any good to tell them to come back down to earth. That's just being hurtful. Keep in mind that these are usually very smart people, probably smarter than you. In their own perception, they value the abstract big picture. This makes them both a valuable part of the team. If you're a nuts an bolts kind of person, you've probably been using extroverted sensing (Se) too much in the meeting. They've got to have time to study all the angles and repercussions in their heads. This takes time; time you may not have.

Now you've got two choices. You can vibe with them and their highly developed extroverted intuition (Ne), or you can code switch to introverted sensing (Si). (Full disclosure - Ne is my blind spot, so there's no way I could change to that language. It would drive me insane. It is a viable solution, but I would have to go with Si, even though it's the tertiary function.) Si is a memory driven function that takes in concrete details in real time and subconsciously compares them to the past, or the way things ought to be. Code switching in this situation is a gentle tether rooting the INTP and INFP to the real world, pulling them back down to cohabitate with the rest of us. Using gentle reminders with words like, "We should be doing this," or, "It should have been done like that," is a good way to ground these two personality types in a more productive manner, and to get them to switch into power mode. Believe me, you haven't seen anything until you've seen someone with an IXFP personality type fully committed to a mission.

If the INTP comes to you upset, she will be like the ISTP in the earlier chapter, caught in an Fe grip. With this personality type, however, your language should have the opposite attitude. This means that your words should come from an Si framework instead of Se. You should be discussing details as concretely as possible with a healthy respect for the past and the way things ought to be. INTP's value that kind of thinking.

The INFP, when upset, will be like the ISFP, caught in a Te grip. Again, Si is your best bet with this personality type. Find a way to strike agreement with your colleague based in the way things ought to be. Use concrete details without flourishes of descriptive language. This should have a grounding a soothing effect, and should help you navigate through the situation in an amicable way.

7. The Fe Blind Spot
Well, it may have escaped your notice, but life isn't fair.

-Severus Snape

Next we have of he most common types (relatively speaking). We also have perhaps the most misunderstood type. The following two personalities both have extroverted feeling (Fe) being in their blind spots. Fe is the function that keeps you in tune with the mood and ambience of the tribe. Granted, the two types in question have a healthy helping of introverted feeling (Fi) in their tertiary slot, but they are oblivious to the social ebb and flow, morale wise, of the outside world. For the INSPECTOR, the ISTJ, compensation is made by a fervent stick-to-the-rules attitude. For the MASTERMIND, the INTJ, coping is more than accounted for by their incredible ability to plan far into the future. For the record, they don't usually mind being awkward. It's often part of their charm.

A great example of the ISTJ personality type is Severus Snape from the Harry Potter books and movies. He's the perfect, dedicated foot soldier who's willing to sacrifice everything to defeat the dark lord. A lot of people have mistyped him because he fits the stereotypes (these are necessary in the MBTI community) of an INTJ. But this character cares about the rules and is motivated by love and dedication to the memory of Harry's mother, a completely introverted sensing (Si) trait.

The reason why the INTJ is often so misunderstood is partly due to their stereotypes, especially when it comes to entertainment . Fictional characters like Sherlock Holmes' Moriarty, James Bond's Dr. Know, and Breaking Bad's Walter White are vivid and memorable examples seen in Hollywood or found in literature. It's plain to see that they are all quite villainous, even Mr. White. The INTJ has the reputation of being Machiavellian in nature, but this only means they are willing to make tough decisions in life. To be great, after all, is to be misunderstood. So let's clear the air. The INTJ isn't interested in causing you any harm. They're just not thinking about you that much.

What would a conflict look like with the two types that have extroverted feeling for a blind spot? Well, it would be awkward. This doesn't mean, however, that they would be wrong. In fact, the odds of being correct are usually in their favor. They are both high extroverted thinking (Te) users, which is the best field for you to meet them on. It would do you no good to worry about decorum. While they are not necessarily interested in causing trouble, they don't mind as long as they aren't breaking the rules (ISTJ, not INTJ). They are more interested in logic and effectiveness. In other words, they want the current project to work, just like you. Be logical and stick to the facts. You can be frank and blunt, as long as you're not being rude. None of those messy feelings are necessary.

When upset, the ISTJ will be in the Ne grip. He will be worried about all the ways things can go wrong. Extroverted intuition (Ne) is a function that explores and perceives abstract connections in the outside world. Given their tendency to focus on the past and depend on memory, an ISTJ's less developed Ne has the potential to stoke the fears of a person's subconscious. Code switching to Te or Fi is your best bet. Be logical without being contradictory with your language. It's also a good idea to recognize his inner values as well as his dependability. The ISTJ is a good soldiers, and should be appreciated and valued.

The INTJ's Inferior function is extroverted sensing (Se). Much like her INFJ cousins, THE MASTERMIND would likely be upset about smaller concrete details going awry and messing up the big plan. This can put her in a dark place. An INTJ friend of mine described life during the 2020 COVID-19 shutdown in stark terms, looking down a large abyss when thinking about the future. The INTJ plans things far ahead into the future, decades ahead. When those plans can no longer be trusted, her very foundations may have been shaken. Once again, code switching to Te and Fi is the way to go. It's important to use logical and affirming language. Remember, just because someone's in a bad way, this doesn't mean that she is stupid. You should be authentic and thoughtful, not condescending. Most types, but especially this one, will know this and appreciate it.

8. The Fi Blind Spot

I haven't failed. I've just found ten thousand ways that won't work.

-Thomas Edison

Before we continue, it must be stated that having introverted feeling (Fi) as a blind spot does not mean that the following personality types do not have inner core values. Personality types with the Fi blind spot certainly do have them just as abundantly as anyone. It's just that communicating with them trying to use that particular kind of language is sure to have virtually no effect. The ENTP, aka THE DEBATER, and the ESTP, or THE NEGOTIATOR, will not be deterred by platitudes, guilt trips, or mission statements. They will say what they want to say, and often know how to get what they want too.

Okay, you've stepped in it. You've got two members of your team (hopefully not at the same time) that you're having to contend with in a meeting. The main thing you need to know is that no matter how brutal they may seem, they are in all likelihood not bearing you any ill will. Also, they are thoroughly enjoying themselves. The first one (ENTP) is exploring possibilities, and stopping him is like putting out a wildfire. Just as soon as you snuff out one spot, three more pop up. The other one (ESTP) is making direct, targeted cuts into any argument that you happen to be making, and it hurts. This is extroverted intuition (Ne) and extroverted sensing (Se) at work. Not only that, but you would also be wise to understand that they both have these skills sharpened through their secondary function, introverted thinking (Ti). Like I said, you've stepped in it.

It's time for you to code switch. Introverted thinking (Ti) is your best bet. Use logic. Sound, workable theories backed up by observable (or at least well known) facts are your friends. Your language must be calm and rational. Both of the EXTP's have Fe as their tertiary function, so pay attention to the atmosphere in the room. They certainly are. Use the feelings of the other people in the room to your own advantage if you must. Remember, they are not interested in being hurtful. They both respect logic and truth, and would prefer an amicable solution for everyone involved. Of course if you're wrong, they are going to win.

If truly upset, the ENTP will be caught in the grip of his inferior function, introverted sensing (Si). He will be talking about details, wrong or right, that don't match up with the past or the way things ought to be. Remember not to insult his intelligence. Keep in mind that Ti is his secondary function. You are better off speaking with Fe, or the harmony language. Reminding him of his importance to the tribe is probably a good way to go.

The ESTP will be caught in a Ti grip. Her introverted intuition will be causing her to jump to dark conclusions. Her gut will be telling her how everything is wrong in the world. Again, code switching to Ti may be difficult. Fe is your best resource here. Remind her of the positive influence she wields and of the great value she has to the tribe . Help her to recognize and remember how she makes things better for her colleagues.

Both THE DEBATER and THE NEGOTIATOR have Ti in the secondary slot of their cognitive stacks. It will be okay to switch into that language eventually, but cold hard facts are not what one would call comforting. Like the famous conservative pundit, Ben Shapiro says, "Facts don't care about your feelings." Plus there is another phenomenon likely at work called looping. If a person is caught in an inferior grip, it is likely that their secondary function is being misused, for lack of a better term, to support the inferior function's misgivings. This creates a feedback loop. That's why I recommend going to the tertiary function. This function, by nature of its position, sees things in a different light. This can sometimes help the person get out of that looping pattern. By the way, looping is a phenomenon found in all personality types, not just the ones in this chapter.

Sometimes, regardless of looping, it would be better to go straight to the secondary function. Usually this is when said function is perceiving in nature. Perceiving functions are opened to change by definition. I believe it's safer to switch to feeling functions too. No research to back that up, by the way. It's just my introverted intuition at work.

9. The Si Blind Spot

As I always say, make mistakes, make mistakes, make mistakes! It's the best way to learn something.

-Ms. Frizzle

The ENTJ and the ENFJ are known as THE EXECUTIVE and THE MENTOR respectively. They are also called THE FIELD MARSHAL and THE TEACHER. These are forward looking personality types, often focused on the future. They spend very little time dwelling on the past. It's no wonder that they share the memory motivated cognitive function, introverted sensing (Si), as their blind spot.

If the ENTJ is giving you flack, odds are he is your boss. Regardless, this personality type is used to calling the shots, and is by no means blind to most of the possibilities of any given scenario. If you've been talking about how things have been done in the past or the way things ought to be, you've been wasting time, both yours and his. It's time to code switch. That having been said, you have two options. You can go with introverted intuition (Ni) if you are privy to some possibilities that THE EXECUTIVE may have missed, which is unlikely. The second option is extroverted sensing (Se). You will need to make your case by painting a picture with vivid sensory details. Paint a picture of success for him. Good luck.

If you're having trouble with the ENFJ, this one is thinking about the feelings and values of the tribe as they all move forward. Much like their thinker cousins, ENFJ's are not worried about how things have always been done in the past. Once again, your two options are introverted intuition (Ni) or extroverted sensing (Se). Perhaps a combination of the two would be more effective here. It's worth a shot. What would this look like? It would be an in-depth description of what is currently needed, loaded with descriptive sensory details, which you can confirm in good faith, are holding to and concurring with the values of the tribe. Again, good luck.

I made code switching seem impossible with the two personality types above, which is unfair. Anyone can use descriptive language. Likewise, anyone can focus on the future with common values in mind. My point is that if you do not usually do these things, you need to practice. This is the wheelhouse of THE EXECUTIVE and THE MENTOR. It's their world. You're just living in it.

When upset, the ENTJ will be in the grip of his inferior function, introverted feeling (Fi). Introverted feeling centers around personal core values, deeply held beliefs, and inner emotions. An ENTJ in distress will have an uncharacteristic lack of self confidence. He will be wondering who he is and what he's doing in this current situation. Code switching to extroverted sensing (Se) language would be helpful, especially if you have a knack for communicating with good sensory details. Also, the use of introverted intuition will help him to have a more positive focus on the future. Like with all types, contradicting him is not helpful. Likewise, using extroverted thinking (Te), his usual go-to function, is a waste of time. Don't bother telling him what to do.

The ENFJ's inferior function is introverted thinking (Ti). When in the grip of this function, he will be speaking of how the system is breaking down. The stream of thought will be logical, but quite subjective in nature. Emphasis will be put on the wrong things in an overly negative light. Remember, he has not come to you for a debate. Code switching to Se and Ni language would be a far better tactic. Use concrete sensory details with a positive focus on the future.

It's important that one understands the fact that both of these personality types can take in vast amounts of information quickly, and can extrapolate the data to make intuitive leaps of perception. The older they get, the better at it they become. If you're not used to this kind of thinking, it may be hard to keep up. This learning style, for lack of a better term, is why they are such valuable team members, and usually team leaders.

10. The Ni Blind Spot

Education can be painful if you get your finger caught in your binder.

-Peppermint Patty

With extroverted intuition (Ne) being their tertiary function, THE PROVIDER and THE MANAGER are the two personality types having introverted intuition (Ni) as their blind spot. The ESFJ is the ultimate mother type, though plenty of manly men are PROVIDERS too. I can't think of any right now, but that's beside the point. The ESTJ is the MANAGER, with excellent organizational and logical decision making skills. If you are the kind of person who likes to dive deep into the cogs, nuts, and bolts of a situation and propose how to change things for the future, these two types are not the people on your team with scuba gear on the ready. Ni is the cognitive function that focuses on the future and extrapolates data, making large intuitive leaps based on advanced pattern recognition and gut feelings. If this is the language that you are speaking, Ni is their blind spot, and they are not going to hear you. Oh, they are totally going to want to talk with you about that too, by the way.

The PROVIDER is focused on harmony. She makes decisions based on the values and feelings of the tribe. This is quite valuable to have on any team, but she is not going to be able to follow your vibe if you're the type who is primarily focused on the future, or if you're trying to bring change into the organization. This type, largely thanks to her high introverted sensing (Si) is mainly memory driven. She is far more likely to concern herself with how things were always done in the past or the way things ought to be. A well adjusted, highly confident ESFJ may go into mama bear mode if you are bringing about too many changes, though she usually would prefer not to hurt your feelings.

The best tactic to take with the ESFJ is to honor her love for the tribe, in other words, her extroverted feeling (Fe). Try talking in her language. If changes are coming and need to be well implemented, it would behoove you to use her concern for the harmony and happiness tribe to your, and everyone else's, advantage. Use her cognitive abilities and natural insights to keep the morale of the organization high while new policies and procedures are being implemented. Give her authentic tasks that help support the well being of everyone involved. Take the opportunity this person provides, you won't regret it.

The ESTJ is an effective manager. Ne is not overly concerned about your vision for the company, school, or organization. In his mind, that stuff is completely your department. That doesn't mean he won't be supportive, but he thinks you should make the decision and just get on with it already. What he wants to know, or perhaps wants you to ask him, is how to make it all work. Don't let the talents and abilities of a team member like this go to waste. Switch the code to his language, extroverted thinking (Te). If this is not your forte, don't worry. The ESTJ has got you covered. Ask him how to organize the new set up, or how to set up the new system. Believe me, he has already been thinking about it for a while. May as well go with it. It's the smart thing to do.

When upset, the ESFJ (PROVIDER) will be in an introverted thinking (Ti) grip. While this function is logical, it is often subjective in nature, especially when it's in the fourth slot of the cognitive stack, and is not so well developed. She will be stating facts, probably derived from her massive Si memory banks, that are negative in nature. While most of these fact are probably wrong or misguided, it will do no good to contradict someone while in an inferior grip. It's a waste of everyone's time. Instead, try code switching.

Extroverted Feeling (Fe) is her lead function. It's a good idea to remind her how valuable she is to the tribe. Let her know that she and her work is appreciated. While acknowledging that things are never perfect, relate to her all of the positive things that are going on, especially the ones directly related to jet work and contributions.

An ESTJ's inferior function is introverted feeling (Fi). Given that, when he is upset and in the inferior grip, it can easily be seen by observing his body language. While this is true for any type in some ways, it's quite noticeable with THE MANAGER. Since Fi is all about personal inner values, this can be highly detrimental for people who are suddenly calling their entire identities into question. The dichotomy is highly noticeable in an ESTJ, who is usually a dynamo and a fast, confident decision maker. While in this state, he is completely vulnerable, like a small child. He will be seeming to make himself physically small.

The Fi grip language is a complete relinquishing of control of the situation, like being someone stuck alone in a random whirlwind. Suddenly this person is a ship without a sail. Code switching here would probably be most effective in the Si domain. This would involve looking back in the recent past and noting the hard work this person has done. He needs to know that the system may be broken, but it can be fixed, and he can help with that.

Of all the inferior grips in the MBTI personality system, introverted feeling seems (in my opinion) to be the most taxing, causing the most fragility. One may be tempted to use tough love, especially given the extroverted thinking (Te) behaviors usually characteristic of the types in it. These are usually take charge kinds of personalities. That having been said, it is still not helpful to be disagreeable with someone while in an inferior grip. Listen to him and use language that lets him know how valuable he is in an authentic way.

In the spirit of full disclosure, I would like to say that one of my parents is an ESTJ. I have had close working relationships with several ESTJs as well. This fragile Fi body language is something I have personally noticed when it comes to this personality type, regardless of gender. I don't know that this phenomenon has need observed in psychological circles or in the MBTI community, but it's something that I've come to know to be true. There are several resources available, especially online in the personality psychology community that discuss the link to body language and cognitive functions. That having been said, I'm currently not aware of resources linking body language and the inferior grip.

11. The Ti Blind Spot

Being dirty is practical. I'm never bothered by girls or mosquitoes.

-Pigpen

THE ENTERTAINER and THE CHAMPION, also known as ESFP and ENFP respectively, are two outgoing, often fun loving, members of any team. However, since they have extroverted thinking (Te) in the third slot of their cognitive stack, that means introverted thinking (Ti) is their blind spot. So if you're a nerd (INTP) or a mechanic (usually ISTP), they may have a tough time sitting in one place and listening to you babble on about tons of information or worse, data. You are not talking their language.

Full disclosure before I continue here. My best friend growing up was an ESFP. Currently I have close working relationships with a few ESFPs too. In the beginning of my career, my mentor was an ENFP. I have a lot of love and respect for both of these two personality types. To me they seem to be underestimated and all too often undervalued. Why would that be? Because they are usually so fun to be around. What can I say? Being enthusiastic comes with a price. But like all personality types, there's a lot more to these people than meets the eye.

If you have these two personality types attending a professional meeting, you literally have a captive audience. You lost them at hello. It doesn't matter how much information you have to give them. They simply don't and really can't care. This doesn't mean that they are dumb - far from it. The ENFPs have all kinds of information bouncing around in their heads already. Your words are just a few menial tidbits entering the melee and competing for their very divided attention. The ESFPs care more about what everybody's wearing, the look on someone's face, or the bad lighting in the room. Beyond that, both types are high introverted feeling (Fi) users. This means that they are far more likely to make decisions based on feelings and values, not your elegantly designed logical arguments. Sorry, they're just not that into you. Moreover, they are just itching to get out of that meeting so that they can finally go get some things done. You're just wasting time, theirs and yours.

So how do you make this a productive meeting? Of course I'm going to bring up code switching here, but I would also recommend utilizing their skills in a different way. They are doers, not listeners. Find a way to make them active participants when meetings are necessary. If you can do this, you won't regret it. ESFPs know how to have a good time. If you're going to have a meeting, may as well have fun, right? ENFPs are great at presentations. They can make people truly feel the impact what's going on and even rally them behind a given call to action. Both types are great at organizing events too. Don't let these talents go to waste.

Okay, back to code switching. There are two great options. The first is introverted feeling. If you're talking about personal values and feelings, they're listening. The second is extroverted thinking (Te). I would be remiss to say that these types are not logical. They are totally logical and rational people, especially when focused on the outside world. They're great organizers and effective planners when they put their minds to it. It only that, but they are really effective at keeping a team motivated. Make them your go-to members when it comes to that. Get them to focus on the system and their integral role within it from a values perspective.

Before moving on to the inferior grip, it should be noted that I am drawing a bit of a caricature. I'm using the stereotypes attached to the personality types. In the personality community, stereotypes are not considered bad things. They are necessary descriptors to help with personality type recognition. To be honest, I've sat in faculty meetings with ESFP and ENFP coworkers who kept themselves better engaged with the proceedings far better than I was at the time. Even so, the descriptions still apply for the most part, and are good rules of thumb to follow.

When upset, the ENFP will be in the grip of his inferior function, introverted sensing (Si). This function is memory driven and concerns itself with the past or the way things ought to be. Being the least developed function in the stack, Si will be focused on how everything, with specific details, is going wrong. Focus on introverted feeling (Fi). Up build your ENFP coworker with authentic praise based on those strong core values. Authentic is the keyword here. Remind him why he's called THE CHAMPION.

By the way, there are two great famous ENFP examples to look at when you have time. Both are television characters. Michael Scott from THE OFFICE is a great example of a dumbed down ENFP. Pigpen from the Peanuts franchise is a great study of a younger version of this type. Remember, these versions of the ENFP are exaggerated for comedic effect. Most of them are smarter than Michael and cleaner than Pigpen.

While THE CHAMPION is focused on specific details in the inferior grip, THE ENTERTAINER is focused on patterns that making thing go awry. This is because the ESFP's inferior function is introverted intuition (Ni). The conversation won't be random, like with Ne, but will consist of how many things are breaking down the system. Instead of being rooted in memory (Si), the conversation will be focused on the future, but in a negative way. This will involve dark predictions of things to come.

Switch the code; change the language. The secondary function in THE ENTERTAINER's cognitive stack is introverted feeling (Fi). Again, authentic praise based on inner core values is important here. You simply must be truthful. You're wanting to navigate, not manipulate. Just because the ESFP is fun loving and outgoing, that doesn't mean she is stupid. Being flattering or condescending is a colossal waste of time, and it can do harm to your relationship.

Another thing to consider with ESFPs and their thinker cousins, ESTPs, is a technique called anchoring. At least, I think that's what it's called. Give me a little latitude here. I'm going way back to my college days when I took an addictionology class. The professor, a practicing psychologist, told the class about how his colleague sometimes had to anchor him back to reality after some particularly intense therapy sessions with severely troubled patients. He would have to tell him things like, "It's okay. You're here in the room with me, sitting in front of my desk. You are in a comfortable chair." Now, I don't know all the particulars of the technique, but it's easy to see the extroverted sensing (Se) connection being made here. If either of these two personality types are truly distraught, they would, in all likelihood, respond to an anchoring technique. Again, this isn't the time to be condescending or contradictory. These personality types lead with extroverted sensing (Se). It's a language they speak fluently. They are picking up on details that are probably not even on your radar. But if you're in a pinch, anchoring may be a handy tactic to take.

12. Your Blind Spot

As long as you think only of yourself, you'll never find happiness. You've got to think about others.

-Schroeder

Now it's time to turn the proverbial tables. This short book was written to help you get through personality conflicts as they arise in the workplace, your home life, or even in school. It must be stated, however, that you have a blind spot too. For that matter, you also have an inferior function. Just as you must navigate through your life dealing with other people and all their eccentricities, those people in turn have to deal with you. You're not perfect, you know? This writing was composed only to help you get a slightly unfair advantage over others, but not in a negative way. The intent in these pages is to help make the reader's life better using simple strategies based on the MBTI system. Truth be told, it is my opinion that everyone would benefit from this knowledge. A rising tide lifts all boats.

Although we didn't dive head first into the complexities of the MBTI system or discuss Carl Jung's psychological theories, I recommend that you do. Sure, you have a lot to do, but it would definitely be worth it. I'm not talking about taking an intense course or reading a ten pound volume. You should consider finding your own personality type, though. It doesn't even have to be MBTI. There are other avenues to take on this journey, like the Enneagram or the Big Five. MBTI is the most accessible and useful to my mind, but regardless of the system, you should learn more about yourself and why you do all those crazy things you do.

Let me explain. I'm not suggesting that you are a slave to your personality type. Far from it! However, the patterns ARE there and you ARE using them, whether you know it or not. Why not find out what those patterns are and use them to your own (and really to everyone else's) advantage?

Using myself as an example, I know that I'm an ISTP. This means that I lead with introverted thinking (Ti). It also means that my blind spot is extroverted intuition (Ne). I know that I won't be too helpful in a brainstorming session. Sure, I've got plenty of ideas, but my idea will be the only, or at least the best solution, to my mind. It's just how I'm wired. Jumping from one topic to another will cause me to zone out, sometimes resentfully. I also know that my inferior function is extroverted feeling (Fe). So if I'm in my inferior grip, I can recognize the language that's going through my mind and perhaps get out of the grip myself. Moreover, I'm a 5w4 in the Enneagram system, so I also know a lot about my internal motivations, and even my psychological Achilles heal. These are good things for me to know, and you should know them about yourself too. You don't have to share them with the world like I have, but you should at the very least find out about them.

Okay, why should you know these things? The main reason in my view is that you can live your life more deliberately. If you're not into personality psychology, that's fair enough. But up until now you've just been floating around your environment without direction when it comes to dealing with and understanding others. You been bumping into others, making mistakes, and stepping on toes, often times quite unconsciously. Now you understand that we are all different some deep, fundamental ways. Not everyone thinks like you. Now you have some rudimentary tools to navigate through your world in a more graceful way. If you feel like they've helped, like I believe they have, you should invest in a few more, get a few more arrows in that quiver. There's no time table, and you don't have to be an expert. But you are bound reap some benefits.

13. Looping

So there I was, all finished with this little book. The beta readers gave me their input. I'd already finished the second edit. The cover had come in, and it was totally sweet. Unfortunately, something was nagging me. In an earlier chapter, I had mentioned looping. Well, it's just down right rude of me to leave people hanging like that. Looping, or looped thinking, needs some explanation. One more brief chapter would be in order.

What is looping? In short, it's a type of habitual thought pattern. We all do it, but it's different for each personality type. While not inherently negative in nature, this phenomenon can be problematic communication wise. The best way to explain it would be to use an example personality type. Sorry folks, I'm going to talk about myself again.

The ISTP has four main cognitive functions, introverted thinking (Ti), extroverted sensing (Se), introverted intuition (Ni), and extroverted feeling (Fe). Looping usually happens when a person is stressed. Of course, a stressed person wants to stay in his comfort zone, so the ISTP isn't going to leave his nice, comfy introverted thinking. His other introverted cognitive function, introverted intuition (Ni) jumps in for moral support, creating a feedback loop. So the Ti is analyzing a negative situation in real time, and the Ni is exploring future possibilities in depth and adding to the worry. Over and over, back and forth, the loop pattern continues.

Okay, so how is a loop broken? For the ISTP, the key is to utilize his secondary cognitive function, extroverted sensing (Se). What does this look like in real life? As for me, I decide to go outside and take a walk. This clears my mind and allows me come back to the situation later with fresh eyes.

Like with blind spots and inferior grips, thinking loops can be addressed through code switching. This may not be as accessible to most people, though. That would be due to the fact that two cognitive functions are at play simultaneously, meaning that the person wishing to navigate through these waters would need to be more knowledgeable and experienced with the MBTI personality system. The good news that the phenomenon in question occurs when a person is stressed, not confrontational or distraught. In other words, the waters may be a little choppy, but they're not treacherous.

One more thing, this chapter will be discussing the most common kind of looping, called primary looping. As described above, primary looping involves the primary and tertiary functions. The other looping, secondary looping, involves the secondary and inferior cognitive functions. Secondary looping is far less common, so to paraphrase Seinfeld's Soup Nazi, "No Loop for You!" Okay, here we go.

ISTP - The loop is introverted thinking (Ti) and introverted intuition (Ni). The Ti is analyzing a negative situation and the Ni is throwing out negative future scenarios. Code switch to extroverted sensing (Se), talking about concrete, descriptive sensory details.

ESTP - The loop is extroverted sensing (Se) and extroverted feeling (Fe). The Se is recognizing negative concrete details, and the Fe is noticing the bad effects they are having on the ambience of a situation. Code switch to introverted thinking (Ti), utilizing good old fashioned logic and deductive reasoning.

ISFP - The loop is introverted feeling (Fi) and introverted intuition (Ni). The Fi is filtering out and evaluating aspects and values at the core of a negative situation, and the Ni is projecting those aspects into the future. Like with their thinker cousins, it is wise to code switch to extroverted sensing (Se), using concrete, sensory details.

ESFP - The loop is extroverted sensing (Se) and extroverted intuition (Ne). The Se takes in the concrete details of a negative situation, and the Ne explores all the other seemingly random things that have the potential to go wrong, thus compounding the effects. Code switch to introverted feeling (Fi), talking about deeply rooted core values.

ISTJ - The loop is introverted sensing (Si) and introverted feeling (Fi). The Si is taking in concrete, detailed information and subconsciously comparing it to the past, or the way things ought to be. Fi evaluates the information based on inner core values, giving emotional weight to the thought pattern. Code switch to extroverted thinking (Te), talking about logic, procedural solutions, and solid organization.

ESTJ - The loop is extroverted thinking (Te) and extroverted intuition (Ne). The Te is analyzing how the system is breaking down and how the atmosphere is becoming disorganized. Ne is exploring random connections in the outside world related to the negative situation at hand. Code switch to introverted sensing (Si), using language related to memories and the way things ought to be.

ISFJ - This is one of the most powerful thinking loops, perhaps because of its strong use of memory. The loop is introverted sensing (Si) and introverted thinking (Ti). Si is continually sifting through memory banks and comparing negative situations to the way things ought to be. Ti is analyzing and confirming the logic of those precepts, reinforcing the loop. Code switch to extroverted feeling (Fe), discussing the values and morale of the tribe and how integral the ISFJ is in that respect.

ESFJ - The loop is extroverted feeling (Fe) and extroverted intuition (Ne). Fe is continually taking the temperature of the morale of the tribe in a given negative situation. Ne is recognizing seemingly random connections to the situation and compounding the perceived breakdown. Code switch to Introverted sensing (Si), using memory driven language discussing the way things ought to be.

INTP - The loop is introverted thinking (Ti) and introverted sensing (Si). The Ti is logically analyzing the details and data of a problem or something that has gone wrong. Meanwhile, the Si is comparing all that data to the past or the way things ought to be. One thing I've personally noticed about my friends with this personality type is that this loop can be quite time consuming. That having been said, the solutions they come up with are often rock solid. Code switching to extroverted intuition (Ne) is the way out of this one. Take time to brainstorm and explore random positive possibilities.

INFP - This loop goes down deep with introverted feeling (Fi) and introverted sensing (Si). The Fi filters stressful situations through core values and emotions, and the Si compares the situation in real time to the past or the way things ought to be. Code switch to extroverted intuition (Ne), using language referring to positive connections in the outside world.

ENTP - This is a fast paced thinking loop consisting of extroverted intuition (Ne) and extroverted feeling (Fe). In a stressful situation, the Ne is exploring the outside world, making connections, while the Fe is gauging the ramifications morale wise. Code switch to introverted thinking (Ti) by using concrete, detailed logic.

ENFP - The loop is extroverted feeling (Fe) and extroverted sensing (Se), The Fe notices the ambience and falling morale of a stressful situation, while the Se is backing all of that up with concrete details. Code switch to introverted intuition (Ni), focusing on positive patterns (silver linings?) in the situation and how they will play out in the future.

INFJ - This is a tough loop to break because it's rarely wrong. Intuitive types, especially those leading with intuition as their primary function, have spent their lifetime sharpening that advanced pattern recognition. But they are human like everyone else. The loop is introverted intuition (Ni) and introverted thinking (Ti). The Ni recognized the patterns leading to a stressful situation, while the Ti supports those postulates with cold, hard logic and facts. Code switch to extroverted feeling (Fe), focusing on the morale of the tribe and the INFJ's integral part in it.

INTJ - This is another strong intuition thinking loop. It consists of introverted intuition (Ni) and introverted feeling (Fi). The Ni recognizes negative patterns and comes to accurate future conclusions, while the Fi filters out the decision making aspects of the situation based on strong inner core values and emotions. Code switch to extroverted thinking (Te). Discuss concrete, logical details about how to address the situation, and to prepare for contingencies.

ENFJ - The loop is extroverted feeling (Fe) and extroverted sensing (Se). The Fe takes note of the morale and atmosphere surrounding a negative situation, while the Se is gathering concreted detailed data to support those observations. Code switch to introverted thinking (Ti), discussing concrete logical facts directly related to the problem at hand.

ENTJ - "Just the facts, ma'am." Quotes from Dragnet aside, the loop is extroverted thinking (Te) and extroverted sensing (Se). This is a very cut and dry kind of thinking. The Te is prescribing remedies and organizing the environment in light of the stressful situation, while the Se is gathering concrete facts and information, thus providing support and feedback in the loop. Code switch to introverted intuition (Ni), insisting on thinking long term and focusing on the future.

There is one final caveat that must be noted when it comes to looped thinking. You can't break someone else's loop. Each and every one of us has to break our own loops. Code switching isn't a magical spell that gets people to do whatever you want. It's simply a way to nudge people in the right direction.

Once again, I hope this book nudges you in the right direction too. That is, it helps you to communicate more effectively with your family, coworkers, or anyone else. So put on your sunscreen, take your ginger tablets, and get yourself ready to go sailing in that great big harbor we call life.

Sources:

I loathe books that are written like term papers. Even so, I'm not the person who came up with MBTI, code switching, or looped thinking. I just put these ideas together in a book that I truly believe will be useful to readers in all walks of life. Here are a few resources that I've used through the years after discovering MBTI.

PLEASE INDERSTAND ME II

David Keirsey

Literally any book by Carl Jung

Personality Hacker Podcast

www.personalityhacker.com[1]

There are dozens, if not hundreds, of YouTube channels in the typology community. Some of my favorites are:

Love Who

LiJo

Frank James

There are many, many more good ones out there.

---

1.   http://www.personalityhacker.com

About the Author

Jon Coley lives in Georgia with his wife, daughters, an orange cat, and an eccentric husky. He has taught school for nearly twenty-five years. That's probably what's wrong with him.

Other Nonfiction by Jon Coley

Schooling Abraham: Applying Maslow's Hierarchy of Needs in Our Schools

From the Peanuts Section: How a Personality Psychology Nerd Sees Education

The Not So Great Divide: Exploring the Femininity to Masculinity Spectrum of Personality

Mini Theses: Rubrics for Writing about Reading (Workbook for schools - Grades 1 through 5)

Middle Grade Fiction, Chapter Books, and Joke Books For Kids
by Jon Coley

The Curse of Mr. M's Castle
  The Other Curse of Mr. M's Castle
  The Fish Creek Forum Volume 1
  The Bookworm
  All Grandpas Fish
  Skate or Die Jacob Jones
  Was That Some Kind of Joke?
  Chuckle Worthy Jokes For Kids
  Is That Supposed to Be Funny?
  Funny Jokes For Kids
  Limerick City
  Funny Poems for Kids

Young Adult Fiction:
  The Echo Chamber
  (A Young Adult Dark Fantasy Series
on Kindle Vella)

Contact Information:

www.joncoleyauthor.com[1]
www.Amazon.com/author/joncoley[2]
facebook.com/Jon[3] Coley Author
Instagram @joncoleyauthor

---

1.   http://www.joncoleyauthor.com

2.   http://www.Amazon.com/author/joncoley

3.   http://facebook.com/Jon

Don't miss out!

Visit the website below and you can sign up to receive emails whenever Jon Coley publishes a new book. There's no charge and no obligation.

https://books2read.com/r/B-A-OVTX-PREJC

BOOKS 2 READ

Connecting independent readers to independent writers.